When The Dead Speak

A Paranormal Journey

John Holliday

Copyright © 2017 by John Holliday

ISBN 13: 978 1977538833

ISBN: 10: 1977538835

Dedication

To my brother James Gregory whose life was cut short by ignorance.

To my wife Debbie who changed my life and brought light and love to me when I was lost in darkness.

To my children, Joseph, Nathan, Elizabeth, and Joshua. We never had a lot, but we always had each other.

To my parents and siblings, we were blessed to have each other.

Contents

Debbie and I meeting ghosts at a cemetery.

Introduction

If I have learned anything about the paranormal; it's that we know almost nothing about it.

Everything can be summed up as either personal experiences, coincidences, or unknowns.

Those that think they have a genuine knowledge or who claim to be experts in a paranormal field are practicing self deception and deceiving others as well.

The truth is as sharp as a knife and as blunt as being hit with a stone from a sling. We know almost nothing about spirits, ghosts, life after death, etc.

Everything we know is speculation.

A lot of what I thought I knew came from being raised in a Christian home.

Unfortunately, and this is true for all faiths- none of what I have experienced seems to fit into any religious doctrine.

We all eventually die and go to the grave in some form.

But there is a part of each of us that continues to live on. I have no idea for how long and in exactly what form.

I do believe our consciousness continues as energy and we are able to make choices, such as traveling to visit relatives, locations.

But for those who are traumatized,

unwilling to accept their deaths, addicted to drugs, unwilling to let go of an earthly possession or love, or have a fear of divine judgment; they remain here on this plain as earthbound spirits.

These are the ones that paranormal investigators are encountering every day in houses, old buildings, trains, hospitals, etc.

Because they are earthbound spirits a lot of what they say to us is not correct. These spirits have not fully transitioned into the next life and thus they are broken or -if you will- disabled and we should approach them with great care.

Paranormal investigators ask these spirits

about Heaven and Hell when these earth bound spirits have not crossed into the light, so they know nothing about what lies beyond. These spirits are stuck in our world and are what we call ghosts.

They do not know about current events. They may be aware that you have entered into their domain or room. They may even know your name and have the ability to follow you home.

They can exert energy and can pull your hair, push you, or even scratch you.

I have seen these ghosts open doors and cabinet drawers and move a ball across a floor.

A word of warning, if a ghost is aware of current events than you are not dealing with a ghost but a demonic entity, and that's something entirely different.

I have heard them weep and cry for help. I have heard them laugh and yell at me to "Get Out!!"

These are examples of intelligent hauntings with an active earthbound spirit or ghost.

Children who have passed away are different from adults. Children may not realize they are supposed to cross over into the light. They will choose to return to the place where they feel safe or the place where they had fun.

Earthbound spirits of children do the same activities as living children. They run, they giggle, they play, and typically they avoid strangers.

When I have investigated and made contact with earthbound spirits of children, they are always accompanied by at least one adult spirit that watches over them.

Do demons pretend to be the earthbound spirits of children? Yes, but unlike what TV shows would have you to believe, it's extremely rare.

Where investigators and novices get into trouble is when you start to rely on these spirits for your own personal life choices.

Should I marry this person? Take this job? This reliance opens the door for a negative or demonic spirit to gain control.

Here is a quote that I live by:

"Whoever fights monsters should see to it that in the process he does not become a monster. And if you gaze long enough into an abyss, the abyss will gaze back into you."

-        Friedrich Nietzsche

Quite simply put if you walk into the paranormal world and make contact; the paranormal will also make contact with you.

There are four types of people who claim to be paranormal investigators:

The PE: In it for the personal experiences.

The PSE: In it for the validation of religious or spiritual faith and personal experiences.

The Tourist: Screams, giggles, talks loudly and is hated by data collecting investigators everywhere. These people just want to have fun.

Data Collectors: These are the serious investigators. Brings equipment, spends hours data collecting, evp sounds, takes video, and then spends hours more doing evidence review.

The paranormal world feeds all four because now it's all about the money. If you can purchase a ticket from a location then you're good to go; as long as you're not vandalizing, the owners of haunted sites do not care how you spend your evening.

For me, it's always been a PSE with data

collecting motivation. I love seeing and touching the history, making contact with ghosts.

But I have learned you will pay a price. The deeper you go into the paranormal the deeper the debt you owe.

Several people have played a key role in my path as an investigator. My daughter Elizabeth who traveled with me during the early years of investigating.

My son Nathan who I always had to bribe to get him to go with me. He never wanted anything to do with ghosts.

My nephew Jason and I visited every location that was available to us. Jason is a true paranormal investigator.

Finally, my wife Debbie who shares my

love of haunted locations and investigating.

James Gregory

It all seems like a distant dream now; my recollections of a blue-eyed, curly haired brunette boy of maybe five years old, hearing a knock at the front door.

My parents rushing to the front door and clearly, something terrible was happening. But for a young boy of four or five, I was in my own world of imagination and safety.

I had no idea how this night with a simple knock at my front door, would change the rest of my life, and the lives of my parents, and my siblings.

Suddenly, my parents rushed out of the house and they were gone as if taken by a whirlwind.

Later, my parents had returned upset. My mother was crying and broken and I still had no idea why. The mood inside our home was dramatically different.

My siblings and I were rushed off to bed. I shared a bed in the very next room from the main room where the knock at the door had happened.

I could hear a lot of talking, voices all through the night and crying. Something terrible had happened, but I didn't understand any of it.

The next days were a fog of activity, whispers of sadness, anger, and uncertainty. My parents did a good job of keeping me in the dark about what was going on at this time because I remember only bits and pieces.

Our home became full of visitors, relatives, and I remember the anger and the unrelenting sense of loss.

My grandmother from my mom's side of the family was there. She was a beautiful, unique soul and if there was ever an angel on earth she was it.

My grandmother's name was Eula and she brought with her a sense of old world calm and a heavenly hug that made everyone feel better if you would just receive it.

Others were there too with my grandmother; aunts and uncles and everything was busy.

A day came that my siblings and I were taken to a place none of us had visited before. I don't remember too much about it. I remember everyone was so sad and trying to behave as though they weren't.

A man greeted us and at some point, I saw my brother there lying in what I thought was a pool of water. I asked my mom, "Why is Greg in the water?"

The pool was actually my brother lying in a coffin.

Gregory was my brother who was just a little older than me. I had three older brothers and a younger sister. Jerry is the oldest, then Tim, Gregory, myself and then my sister Jane.

"Why is Gregory in the water?" I remember pointing down at him. At this point I remember this upset my parents and I believe my grandmother and my uncle Charlie took me from my parents.

I didn't understand why we were leaving Gregory behind in the water.

The whole incident made me feel very unsafe wondering if one of us might be left behind also.

After this, I remember my mom slept with me for many days to comfort me. I would ask her questions about what happened to Gregory. Sometimes my sister, Jane would ask questions too.

Mom was always very patient with us. I remember mom telling me, "that God wanted Greg's spear so God came and took it."

Now that I am older, I am sure the conversation was quite different, and my child's mind twisted mom's words trying to find understanding.

Mom probably said something like, "God wanted Gregory's spirit in Heaven so God came and took it."

I remembered as a child wondering if God would spear me!

It was a difficult time for me.

Anyway, they say time heals all wounds, but that's a lie. Time doesn't heal all wounds. The wounds are still there, and the tears are still real and as fresh as the moment the events occurred.

Later, as I entered public school I remember that I didn't like school too much. I would have rather stayed home. The teacher was nice enough and the other children, well they were like any other children.

One child bullied me a lot. Once pushing me down in the restroom where I then hit my head under the sink and I had to get six stitches in my head.

My parents and the teacher weren't too happy about that.

After that incident, I was allowed to go to the restroom alone. I remember going in there, not because I needed to go, but because I wanted to talk to Gregory.

I would walk in there and step inside one of the stalls where I would ask Gregory to appear to me. He never did. I would talk to him as though he was standing there with me.

Years later my mother told me that I was so traumatized by Gregory's death that they feared that they would have to put me into therapy.

Another event that happened that probably started me road down the paranormal is one night while sleeping I was awakened by a voice saying "hello."

I thought it was my dad who worked nights and would sometimes wake us up to tell us to "go to sleep" and that he loved us.

As I opened my eyes I looked around and seeing nothing I was confused. Then, a man made of light, waving his hand up and down, walked along the left wall of the room repeatedly saying "hello."

The man was like a shadow cast on the wall but made of light.

He walked with leg movement and the one arm moved waving.

I watched and said "hello" back.

As this figure got closer I panicked and screamed.

Both my parents rushed into the room and I yelled there's a man in my room saying "hello" to me.

My mother rushed to my side and dad searched the area.

Mom said, "It must have been a dream."

Dad said, "I don't see anyone here."

I never saw the light man again. But I know he wasn't a dream.

As I grew older mom explained more about the events of Greg's death to me.

Gregory had left the yard to go play at a friend's house. The friend's dad had left a loaded gun out and unfortunately for Gregory, his life was taken by carelessness.

Greg's friend found the gun and they decided to play cowboys and Indians, or something like that. Regardless, Gregory was shot and killed.

My dad wanted to file charges against the boy's father but none were ever filed. Dad even tried to sue the guy for wrongful death but this guy had nothing so my parents lost their child and received no justice.

Both my parents paid a high price that day for this guy's carelessness.

The year was 1966 long before gun owners were being held responsible.

Cemeteries

As I grew from a boy into a teenager and into adulthood I was always fascinated by cemeteries. The older the cemetery, the better I felt. I felt I could hear the distant and current voices speaking as though carried on the wind right to me.

It wasn't just cemeteries but battlefields and historical places. Sometimes, I could feel the people walking beside me as though I was there with them, as one of them.

Cemeteries were special though, because here I would find a thousand voices from a thousand places and moments in time telling me their stories.

Sometimes these voices were friendly and sometimes they were not.

Visiting battlefields, I could hear a thousand voices, but they were about the battle and their lives as soldiers or missing their families.

Cemeteries taught me that I had to learn how to talk with them from their time and in a way they could understand me.

An example of this is one day my daughter Elizabeth, my nephew Jason and I were visiting John Dillinger's grave at Crown Hill Cemetery in Indianapolis, Indiana.

John Dillinger Jr, is buried in a family plot

there along with his father and other family members.

We were standing by John Dillinger's headstone talking between ourselves wondering about his life of crime and his life.

One of us asked something along the line of "John did you enjoy robbing banks?"

A disembodied male voice spoke out and said "I did it and other will too."

All three of us heard this voice and it was an amazing moment for all of us. We were sure John Dillinger Jr; public enemy #1 had just spoken to us from the grave.

Another example is when I visited tiny Yorktown Cemetery in Virginia. This small almost unnoticed cemetery where a small church once was located, is safely protected inside Yorktown Battlefield National Park.

I walked into this cemetery trying to see if any of the residents there would speak to me.

The minister who is buried there spoke and said to me, "Get back Satan."

It was then I realized I had transgressed in their eyes by not properly introducing myself and my intentions. This minister was still protecting his flock over two hundred years later.

I knew better. I had learned previously how important introductions are when you visit a location. How important it is to make your intentions known.

I have heard paranormal investigators say, "Why would someone who is buried linger in a cemetery?"

The ground is consecrated and by their faith if they believe the ground is hallowed and is their resting place, why wouldn't they?

Do I believe all spirits linger where they are buried? Of course not. Spirits have free will and travel as they will.

Another example from a cemetery is at Crown Hill Cemetery in Indianapolis, Indiana. My daughter Elizabeth went with me this day as we investigated the area near the old gothic chapel.

There we did a ghost box session near a grave of a gentleman that dated back to the Revolutionary War. I recorded a voice that came through that was odd and different from anything I had recorded before.

At home, I listened to it repeatedly without making any type of sense out of it. I just knew it was a voice.

Then, it dawned on me to play it backward. When I played the recording backward I heard a growl and then a deep disturbing voice say "Let me in."

It was creepy and caught me off guard because my first thought was I was dealing with something demonic.

Immediately, I decided well I'm not going back there.

A few days passed and I began to feel guilty and ashamed that maybe I was meant to go back and bless the area.

Perhaps the souls resting there were in bondage to this entity?

I had some baby oil which I prayed over and decided to return to the same place. I was scared but determined to go.

I told Elizabeth I was going and to my surprise, she wanted to go with me.

When we drove up to the area I told her to wait in the car while I did the cleansing. Beth looked at me like I was crazy and said she was going with me.

We approached the area and I was nervous. I said the prayers and touched the blessed oil on as many places and tombstones as I could.

I expected all hell to break loose at any moment. But to my amazement, all was peaceful and serene.

However, I did feel as though we were being watched. Something was there with us, not happy, but powerless to stop us.

As we left I knew I had met a powerful territorial spirit. It wasn't a demon but a human spirit pretending to be a demon.

I also felt gratitude from the nearby black soldiers buried there. I wondered if maybe this territorial spirit was a slave owner or some type of taskmaster still trying to prey on the black souls buried there.

Another example comes from Stepp Cemetery in Martinsville, Indiana.

I used to go there alone a lot; trying to make contact. Pretty much center of the cemetery stands Elizabeth's grave. I would always sit near Elizabeth's grave. I found being near her very comforting.

One day I was there sitting and from my rear, I felt someone approach me. I knew if I turned she would leave.

I heard a young girl say "Poppa."

I could feel she was searching for her father.

In that moment she stepped a little closer and once she realized I wasn't her "Poppa" she vanished.

When I turned around no one was there.

I have learned spirits always seem to approach from the rear. I am not sure why. Perhaps they need to feel safe?

After that event, I would take stuffed animals and candy to Stepp cemetery to leave for the little girl looking for her "Poppa."

The other thing about Stepp cemetery is that there is a not so friendly spirit there. He is a watcher or a guardian. He watches the place; his energy is strong and he wants you to leave.

One night there near baby Earl's grave I received three scratches on my arm. I am sure it was the guardian spirit trying to get me to leave.

Near baby Earl's grave, I have also heard growls. It's not a demon more likely a relative of the infant buried there.

Demons have better things to do than hang out in cemeteries.

Stepp is also a place where the spirits like to play with all things electronic. I have had them turn on my camera, my cell phone, etc.

If you follow the trail behind baby Earl's grave you will come to a small pond. I have often wondered if the Crabites used this pond for their ceremonies.

The pond has a strange vibe and there is a presence to it.

Rumor is, Wiccans and Satanists often visit Stepp to conduct ceremonies.

Yet another example from Martinsville, Indiana is an old Catholic Cemetery that I stopped by on my way home after visiting Stepp.

As I parked my car near the cemetery gate an uneasy feeling came over me. It was that feeling of not being welcomed there.

I was a stranger to all that resided there.

This feeling happens to me a lot at small cemeteries. Perhaps because all the souls in a small cemetery are actually family members or know each other compared to larger city cemeteries.

I paused outside the gate to give the spirits there time to see that I meant no harm. I snapped a few photos with my camera, however, the uneasy feeling did not go away. I thought about leaving but I decided to enter.

As I walked around taking photos I started to record an EVP session.

I felt someone move right up to me from behind, circle around me and pause then move to my right. I felt suddenly very cold as though a frosty wind was blowing right through me. I was trembling, freezing.

Then a male voice spoke to my right ear…"It's c-o-l-d now."

My shivering was almost violent as I dashed back to my car. I was done with this location. Clearly, I was not welcomed here.

After I secured the gate lock and was clear of the cemetery fence I heard an older female voice say "Stay the hell out."

The voice was a lady probably seventy years or older.

My time inside the cemetery was less than five minutes.

About a year would pass before I would dare return to this location. The spirits there had done a good job of freaking me out.

When I returned, I brought gifts of candy. I offered a Catholic prayer before entering and waited out front for a longer period of time so they knew I was there. I also said to them "remember me?"

I still do not think they were pleased but they tolerated me this time.

This was another reminder when visiting locations how important it is to know the story of the people there, what they believe, and to show proper respect.

There is a lot more to cemeteries than disembodied voices and capturing EVPs.

There is the emotion, the sense of loss that every cemetery holds.

For the artist or the lover of art, cemeteries are full of ornate art.

Families who have suffered a loss spare no expense to decorate their departed loved ones resting places with brass, marble, and other fine cut stone.

All you have to do is walk through any larger cemetery to see these ornately decorated statues, mausoleums, and headstones.

Even the older cemeteries feature unique

headstones not found today. Such as the headstones with the hand pointing to Heaven or the infant's headstone with the lamb on top of it.

Sadly, many older historic cemeteries have fallen victim to vandalism.

My personal belief is that paranormal investigators who do not visit cemeteries are missing out on important experiences.

Even if you believe that the deceased spirit would not linger there I believe that the spirit knows that is the resting place his or her family chose and the spirit can choose to return to the location when the site is visited by family members or visitors.

A Singular Event

I was a major gym rat and would spend four to five days a week working out in the gym. The owner of my local gym saw me so much there that he gave me a free membership if I agreed to watch the place for him.

Of course, I agreed because I was already there working out so why not get a free membership?

Sometimes, my sons, Nathan and Joseph would go, and sometimes Elizabeth would go with me.

I spent a lot of money on the right foods and supplements so that I could get the best bang for my workout efforts. One day Nathan and I were heading to the gym and a semi cut us off and I had to drive off the road to keep from hitting the semi. In that moment my life changed forever.

About a week later I was working out in the gym lying on my back lifting dumbbells when my left arms quit working. I had to move my head to keep the dumbbell from striking me. It was a scary moment.

Over the next several days I noticed that I no longer had energy and my hands shook.

I began to suffer blackout moments where I didn't know where I was or how I got there.

I had memory loss. Things I knew that I should remember were just gone.

It was terrifying.

One day I came home from work and told my mother about it. I said, "I was on the highway and I had no idea how I got there. I didn't know where I was."

I just remember that I needed to stay in my lane.

I was getting in trouble at work too. My supervisor was upset because I was falling behind on assignments. But I couldn't remember how to do them. (Even if I had recently worked on them)

Then I would have moments of clarity again. It was unpredictable.

My family doctor sent me to a neurologist.

After several tests, I was diagnosed with seizure disorder. My situation continued to worsen as I lost weight, had trouble breathing at night, etc.

I received a C-Pap machine, a bunch of medications, and disability within ninety days.

All this from what seemed like a small event during a normal day. I thought Nathan and I were fine after being run off the road. My car only had minor underbody damage. But I had hit my head at some point and that was enough to change everything.

I lost a lot of my independence but I gained a higher level of appreciation for life and spirituality. A few days before the wreck mom came to me and said that she had a dream that something bad was going to happen to me, but it was God's will.

Just a footnote. The ancients believed that epilepsy was a curse placed on a person by demons or by one of the Gods.

I can testify this is false. In a way, my epilepsy has been an age of enlightenment for me.

It brought me back to taking spirituality much more seriously. I have greater empathy than ever before.

Burger Chef Murders

As a teen, I remember sitting in our living room at home and unfolding the local newspaper and reading about the Burger Chef murders.

On a Friday night, November 17th, 1978, four Burger Chef employees vanished from their place of business. Their bodies were later discovered in the woods by hunters. This murder case has never been solved.

I was just beginning to investigate the paranormal and I decided to see if I could get any of the four victims to speak to me.

The victims were Jayne Friedt age 20, Daniel Davis age 16, Mark Flemmonds age

16, and Ruth Ellen Shelton age 18.

I still felt a sense of loss from my own brother's death and felt maybe I could bring these families some closure.

Gregory's death would continue to direct my paranormal path for years to come.

Again, my daughter Elizabeth decided to join me on this adventure. Neither of us realized how this paranormal investigation would be different from any other.

The old Burger Chef restaurant still stood there vacant and seemingly forgotten like the four murder victims. It was October, 2011 thirty-three years after the murders and there we were reaching out to the victims trying to resolve the deaths of these four young people.

At that time my favorite piece of equipment was the SBS7 ghost box or as some people called it "a spirit box."

Anyway, we started our session from inside the car. As the session went on the mood inside our vehicle grew heavy and sad. We were not alone.

It wasn't just us there anymore. We felt the four victims were there but others were there too. Some very negative and angry spirits were with us, not wanting us to communicate.

Although the four victims were there, they

didn't want to talk about that eventful night. They wanted their families to know they were alright and that they loved them. They didn't want to give out details about that night because each had moved on.

As the session continued the heaviness grew and Elizabeth became very uncomfortable and wanted to leave. But not me I was captivated by the allure of it all.

Several times Elizabeth pleaded for us to leave with each attempt becoming more desperate.

Finally, we did leave only to drive out to

where the bodies were found in the Timber Heights area.

On the way, we got completely lost and it took us several hours to get there. We were completely out of sync and everything was out of place. The world became upside down and I should have taken us home.

When we finally arrived at Timber Heights I started the second ghost box session as I drove around the now upper scale housing edition.

The heaviness was like drowning in a pool, but I was intoxicated by it.

The events of that fateful night involved two men; one was bigger than the other.

The bigger man was much more violent and brutal.

It seems that the whole thing was about drugs and money. It may have started in the drive through or in the restroom inside the restaurant. Words were exchanged between one of the teenage boys and the men. So the men pulled their vehicle around behind the restaurant and waited for the restaurant to close and when one of the boys opened the rear door to carry the garbage out the men gained entry and the rest is history.

Sadly, I believe two of the teens were dealing drugs from the restaurant. It wasn't a robbery but a killing due to anger from one of the teens smarting off to the wrong guy.

Can I prove this? No, I cannot. Do I know which two teens were dealing….yes I do. Will I name them? No, I won't.

My main reason for this is these voices can and do lie.

This crime will never be solved by law enforcement.

So there we were driving back and forth at Timber Heights feeling the weight of what had happened that night.

We were bathing in sadness and rehashing feelings, emotions that had been dormant for thirty-three years.

We did finally leave the area.

Elizabeth was never as glad as when I headed home and her frustration with me was over the top. I had stayed too long and now I realized it.

Walking through the front door of our home it was immediately clear whatever we had encountered had followed us home.

The sadness we felt, the longing for answers, the longing for life, questions about why, the pain, the hurt, was all still there.

The heaviness that wanted something from us we didn't have the ability to give.

Neither of us slept that night or the next several nights.

Then out of the blue when all hope seemed lost my nephew Aaron called me and said, "Uncle is everything alright?"

I didn't know how to answer this question so I just told him. My nephew Aaron is spiritually wiser than his years would reveal.

I told him about my attempt to reach out to the four murder victims.

Aaron said, "Uncle, you didn't just step into it you basically jumped right into it and now you will have to learn from this and pay the price.”

Is there anything I can do? This is terrible. We can’t sleep and we feel like we are being watched, etc.

“Uncle, when you look into the spirit there is always a price.”

Aaron told me about using protection stones, amulets, and sage. My nephew saved us that day.

Aaron sent me some sage and once I received it I saged our entire house and the heaviness lifted and we were able to sleep.

I always have sage in my home now. I

always have protection stones, healing stones, etc.

Other Unsolved Crimes

Thus began a long period of about six years of intensive paranormal study, spiritual rebirth, and in the end disappointment.

I was determined to see if the paranormal could provide answers to unsolved crimes and bring closures to families. I knew that these spirits existed. I knew the dead could speak and I was certain they would want their crimes solved and their killers captured and brought to justice.

I ventured out once again to see if I could find answers.

I was drawn to two cases Molly Dattilo and Lauren Spierer. Each for a different reason.

A little background on each person:

Molly Dattilo: missing since July 6, 2004, from Indianapolis, Indiana. Date of birth June 13, 1982.

Molly disappeared from the Thorton's gas station 5700 of Crawfordsville Rd and hasn't been seen since.

Lauren Spierer: missing since June 3, 2011, after visiting a Kilroy's pub in Bloomington, Indiana.

I spent endless hours over the next years searching for both girls. Friends and family members even helped me search for them.

There were moments when I thought I was close to solving both cases, only to watch all hope evaporate.

I learned very quickly that not all voices are truthful and the closer you get to knowing the truth the harder the negative, darker spirits work to deceive you.

The one thing I believe is that Lauren is very near water, a railroad and a bridge have something to do with her.

Molly is in a field and her family is on the right track.

I regret not being able to help more.

One day I was walking in a field by White River searching for Molly and I was very near a railroad track and a very kind, gentle spirit came up to me.

She was a young woman, she wanted to say "thank you." She was happy. She was okay she was with her relative again.

I said to her, "But I can't see you."

In a gentle voice, she replied, "I'm sorry,"

She stayed for a moment longer and she was gone.

That was my sign from Molly to stop looking, everything was alright.

It's hard to describe in words moments

like that, when the supernatural greets you.

I still wasn't ready to stop searching for Lauren. Those boys that she was with the night she vanished had rubbed me the wrong way.

Why didn't they take her back to her dorm room?

I continued to search for Lauren spending hours searching in Bloomington and Martinsville. My friend Robin, my nephew Jason, my daughter Elizabeth even helped search.

We looked in the Spring, the Summer, the Fall and the Winter. We waded in creeks and even dug up places to look for her body.

Ghost box recordings revealed words like Walnut Street, McDonald's, Jesse, Cory, and even Wolf.

In the end, I eventually gave up. But I am sure she is near water.

Early on I was searching an area near a lake in Bloomington and I could feel a very sad lost female spirit. This spirit was crying, mournful and ashamed of making poor choices and wanted to tell her family that she was sorry.

She was hurt and although near me she wasn't about to trust me. I knew why. She was an easy read for me. Imagine if the people you had called friends betrayed and abandoned you and these friends happened to be male.

So when I returned to the area I brought Robin with me. I sent Robin off alone with a recorder into the area where I had felt this female presence before.

I felt certain Robin being female and a mother could make contact with this female spirit.

After we left and I got home and listened to the recording sure enough about halfway through you can hear a female corresponding back and forth with Robin. This female spirit is so upset.

I posted the recording on YouTube. I was sure we had just made our first contact with Lauren.

The more I listened to it the more I was heartbroken for this young lady. When we returned to the area I crossed Lauren over. After that, I never really had such strong contact with her again.

Weeks after crossing Lauren over there was a part of me that regretted doing it. She was so ready to talk. But she was so miserable and living as an earthbound spirit that the compassionate thing to do was to release her from the emotional pain she was in.

Not a week goes by that I do not pray for closure for Lauren's family.

Someone at that party that night knows what happened to Lauren and it's time for them to speak up.

Central State Hospital

One of my favorite places to go and investigate was Central State Hospital in Indianapolis, Indiana. Central State was a former Psychiatric Hospital for the insane that was abandoned by the state in 1994.

At one time the hospital covered over one hundred acres of ground and had its own chapel, several buildings to house patients, a bowling alley, a bakery, fire house, cannery, and gardens with fountains. The largest building, known as the Seven Steeples, housed the female patients.

The whole area housed about 3,000 patients and was for the most part self-sufficient.

By the time I started to explore the property the Seven Steeples building had long since been torn down and most of the buildings were in decay.

The main buildings still standing were Bolton, Evans, and Bahr, with Bahr the one used to house the most violent. The carpentry building, the old power plant, administration and what is now the Medical Museum building is all that was left of the once mighty hospital.

There was also rumored to be about five miles of underground tunnels that connected each building that remained.

The only building not suffering from decay is the Medical Museum building which operates as a museum and does active tours and preserves the history of this historic location.

Tour guides from the Medical Museum will eagerly tell you "There are no ghosts here."

Well from my experiences exploring the buildings and tunnels, I beg to differ.

I remember sitting in my car inside the small park at the corner of West. Vermont and North Warman St and looking towards all the structures and the fence that surrounded the abandoned hospital property.

I remember thinking, "How am I going to slip into this gigantic place?" My good friend at the time and fellow paranormal investigator Emily was with me.

The size of this place seemed overwhelming and somewhat foreboding to me. I had never attempted any investigation or any exploration of a site so large and decayed.

Emily was excited and ready to charge in and see what we could find. I was much more cautious.

I could see even from a great distance that many of the buildings were in bad shape. Most of their windows were broken out, doors hanging loose, and I genuinely wondered if it was safe to venture inside.

As an asthma sufferer, I worried about the air quality and breathing in dust and others things into my already straining lungs.

The place also had an ominous vibe that spoke of sadness, a longing of stories and dreams never fulfilled and a warning to stay away.

I felt the siren's call to enter, but I also knew the story behind the Greek myth.

Emily grew impatient with me as I wavered.

She pointed out several broken areas in the surrounding fence where anyone could easily enter the grounds without being seen.

So after much internal battling, we ventured towards the downed fence. We came in through the fence area where Evans and Bolton stood.

I remember it was a warm day and the breeze blew across my face. The trees cast strange shadows on the ground and on the buildings. I wondered what this place must have looked like in its splendor with staff and patients everywhere.

Once on the grounds, it was like walking on a different planet. The buildings were marked with graffiti and I felt like we were being watched from inside every building around us.

I also expected the police or security to chase us away at any moment.

The first thing I noticed was that Evans and Bolton were twin buildings. They were identical in building design. At least that's how it appeared to me from the outside.

Staring through the broken glass windows and seeing the dangers of sharp glass and metal objects hanging down from the roof I knew I would enter each building.

I wondered if we would bump into homeless people or drug addicts.

My greatest fear was that we would encounter moronic teenagers or gang members.

I can't remember which building Emily and I entered first, but it was either Evans or Bolton. It was dark, full of dust, probably asbestos, and dangerous because of sharp objects hanging out of the walls, the ceiling, and the floor.

My guess is we had entered the Evans building.

Neither of us wore masks and looking back this was a huge mistake that aggravated my breathing problems.

I could taste the dust in my mouth and throat.

When I shined my flashlight I could see dust and plaster particles flying through the air.

Both Evans and Bolton were three-story structures. The basement area led to the tunnels which connected each building.

The main floor was in very bad shape.

vandals had gone in and ripped out anything of value. Copper pipes, wiring, etc. This was a pattern repeated in every building.

There were also signs of vandalism just for the sake of it.

There were still paintings on the walls around the family areas and the nurse's stations. Individual's rooms still contained personal items. Curtains still hung on certain windows.

It was here that I heard a voice say, "You're not allowed to be here."

I looked around and no one was there. Emily was off exploring another area.

Someone didn't like that I had invaded their once private quarters.

Everywhere you could feel life as though the place had never been abandoned. The laughter, the tears, the hope and their nightmares all right there with me.

I can't lie, there were moments when I felt like I was prying into someone's personal space and I half expected to see a patient in a gown staring back at me.

After a few minutes, the voices in my head became too much and I had to get out of the building. Emily thought I was having an anxiety attack.

It was as though I was a stranger and they were alarmed by my presence and screaming at me to leave. The voices causing my mind to swirl in a storm of unease to where I just had to escape or face their assault.

I quickly made my way back to where we entered and left the building by squeezing through the opening in the door.

Emily and I walked back the way we came across the field and back to our vehicles.

We then drove around to West Drive and parked by the Medical Museum to get another view of the location.

As I drove down West Drive there is a small patch of trees by where the Indiana State Police now graze their horses. The trees had a strange and powerful magnetic pull to them and I knew we were being watched.

I found out later that this area is an unmarked cemetery where residents were buried without headstones or ceremony. This is known as Section #1 according to Findagrave.com.

I felt hundreds of people watching us.

I wondered if these patients who were abandoned by their families and left to wilt and die at Central State and then buried without love or dignity were secretly used by hospital staff to train other doctors.

Was there active grave robbery going on at Central State Hospital at some point in its history?

An interesting tidbit that may give a clue is that during the Medical Museum Tour that I have taken twice now. One of the tour guides described how physicians would hire people to steal bodies.

After the burial, the thieves would dig into the graves and break into the coffin. Then they would insert a large metal fish hook just under the deceased person's chin and pull the body out.

It was quite profitable and illegal.

The other cemetery is near Tibbs and West Washington St, South of Mount Jackson Cemetery. This is sections #2, #3 and #4 per Findagrave.com.

A not so elegant memorial stands there

now. A sad monument to remember forgotten souls.

There is also a tunnel entrance nearby here although I never found it.

I have heard rumors of another unmarked cemetery on the grounds of Central State Hospital.

I don't know if it's true.

But I am sure things were done in darkness here that we will never know about.

In about a week we were back at Central State. We returned to the Evans buildings. This time my nephew Jason was with us.

Our goal for this trip was to get a look at one of the rumored tunnels. Jason and

Emily would explore the tunnel while I did look out from our vehicle.

We were nervous because while pulling into the area we noticed police cars cruising around.

Jason and Emily loaded up with video equipment, flashlights, emf detectors and off they went. I pulled around to a good location where I could see any approaching cars.

After about thirty minutes my cell phone alerted me they were ready to come out. "Was the coast clear?

"Yes," I drove right next to the building and they rushed to my vehicle and we drove away.

They were so excited about all they had seen. I was excited to get home and download the video and review it.

At home, we watched our new evidence. It was clear that despite popular rumor the tunnels were never used to transport patients from building to building. The tunnels were cramped, filled with vast networks of plumbing and not clear enough for any type of wheelchair or gurney.

The tunnels were primarily used by maintenance workers and maybe employees who dared to get from building to building.

Our conversation now shifted to another popular rumor that patients who acted out were sometimes chained to a wall in the dark in a certain area inside one of the tunnels. I was determined to locate this spot. We figured it must have been near the Seven Steeples, Medical area.

The problem was we knew Seven Steeples and the Medical area no longer existed. But, perhaps the tunnel going there was still intact and this location could be found.

The next day Jason and I returned to Central State to explore more of the buildings. This time we didn't see the police cruising about.

We drove past the former administration building, boiler room, power plant, carpentry building and theatre.

We parked right next to the administration building and sat in my car for a few moments making sure that we were in plain sight of anyone watching. That way if the police were around and wanted to chase us off we hoped they would do it before we entered the building.

We walked around taking photos. Jason and I taking turn posing and snapping each other pictures. Once we were sure everything was safe we entered the building.

Jason is his own investigator and soon we were separated each captivated by different areas of this huge building. The main floor had papers, items thrown around everywhere. But unlike Evans the building was in decent shape.

In a few moments just as we were slowly moving through the first floor we began to hear noises.

I thought, "Raccoons?" It didn't sound like anything a human.

Jason came rushing back to me and asked, "Is someone else here with us?"

We paused and neither of us made a sound as we listened for any noise.

We heard nothing.

Just as we started to relax and start our investigation again we heard noises again.

Panic ran through us as we were sure we were about to meet drug addicts, gang bangers or the police.

Small banging sounds, as though it wanted our attention then silence.

Then we heard what sounded like very loud footsteps coming from the floor right above us.

We fled the building.

I am certain we were the only living people inside that building that day.

We ventured over to the boiler building. The door had been pried open so we entered easily. Old tools were scattered on the floor.

It was dark and dank and you had to

watch your footing unless you trip over an item lying on the floor.

We spent a few minutes snooping about observing everything inside before making our way to another tunnel entrance.

Down some metal stairs and there stood another tunnel. We were excited for the opportunity to see where it would lead us.

As we walked this short tunnel it became clear that all the tunnels had the same appearance and there were signs on the walls informing you which way to certain buildings.

It was strange these signs showed the way to the chapel and other buildings that no longer existed.

There was the now all too familiar sound of dripping water from leaking and badly rusting plumbing. The air was cold and if your flashlight lost power it would be near impossible to find your way back out.

Central State was grabbing hold of us. It was a love affair with the location, the history and the many ghosts that lingered there.

Over the next few years, everyone that I took to Central state fell in love with it.

Little did I know the best was yet to come.

Central State Hospital II

About this time, I joined a paranormal meetup group so that I could explore even more haunted places. At first, I really enjoyed the group. We went to Fox Hollow Farms, Whispers Estate, and the Gas Light Inn.

One night, while at the group meeting we were discussing where we should investigate next.

I suggested Central State Hospital.

That suggestion unfurled a thousand questions about bumping into homeless people, drug addicts, and of course the police. Central State was after all still considered private property and patrolled by the police.

Eventually, one person in our group contacted someone she knew and received permission for our group to enter the property.

When that day came so many people showed up that it was a sight to see. Cars were lined up to get in and we had to park them in several different areas inside the property.

If someone had turned Central State into a paranormal attraction they would have made a lot of money.

I passed out masks to each person in the group. I knew the level of plaster dust, etc.

they would encounter. In a few moments people broke into teams and off they went. At least one person in each team carried a firearm.

I showed them how and where to enter the buildings, and where to find each tunnel. By this time I knew the layout really well.

On this trip I entered the Bolton building and spent most of my day here. Curtains still hung in certain rooms. Personal items inside some of the rooms. Pictures still in frames, clothing, towels, and patients' medicine lying about.

Just like Evans the level of destruction from vandals was appalling. Pipes torn out from the walls and ceiling. Glass broken out of windows and doors. Graffiti marking everything.

It was now that I realized the ghosts here were still living here as patients, and they were becoming more accepting of me.

At first, they were wary of me because I was a stranger and they had seen others come and do great damage.

But I hadn't damaged anything or taken anything. In fact, I spent a lot of my time talking to them and now they were listening.

I was one of them.

I also decided at this moment I would give no more large tours of Central State Hospital.

I no longer felt unsafe there. I felt like they would watch out for me. It was weird.

I wanted to hear their story. I wanted them to speak to me and touch me. I wanted to touch them.

Not all the ghosts there were friendly; many were confused, angry and sick. But none of them wanted to hurt me. Mostly, they just wanted others to leave them alone.

The only thing that I continued to fear was the living. Central State Hospital property is located in a high crime area of Indianapolis.

There were still buildings to explore. I knew I needed to film them all before they were gone. I had this nagging feeling that everything would soon be erased and even the ghosts there would be forced to leave.

The funny thing is, they knew it too. They just wanted to be remembered.

Central State Hospital III

Over the next several months I explored virtually every inch of Central State hospital. But I was especially drawn to one building.

The Bahr building was unique from the other residential buildings at Central State because it housed and treated the more violent patients.

This building was also shaped differently from Evans and Bolton.

Bahr had metal cage doors and metal beds clearly those locked inside were considered a threat to society. It was also apparent there were levels of security inside the building from low risk to higher risk patients.

I had no idea that this building and its inhabitants would be connected with me from this point on.

I remember entering the building one day and while doing an EVP session asking, "Do you want to go outside with me?"

The answer was decisive... "We are not allowed."

Although the building stood abandoned for twenty plus years the ghosts inside still lived in its walls and acted as though the staff, the rules and everything they knew still existed.

I asked, "Is anyone in pain?"

I always got a "Yes."

They never knew anything about current events nor did they want to discuss it.

But asking about events inside that building during that time period of their stay, I could get a response.

One event that really stands out is Jason was in town so he and I ventured out to

Central State and immediately entered the Bahr building.

As was our normal we separated each to explore on his own. In a few moments, Jason came rushing back towards me saying he was hearing strange noises coming from a certain area. He wondered if other people were in the building.

We headed that way to see.

As we approached Jason pointed to the resident's door where the strange noises were coming from. Fortunately for us, my IR camera and emf detector was on and running so we captured the entire moment.

The door was slightly cracked just enough to glimpse inside. We could see a shadow moving around inside. This was Thanksgiving Day and we were wondering is this apparition here seeking his or her Thanksgiving dinner?

As I pushed the door open the shadow vanished and the noises stopped. The EMF detector sounded as we entered the room. We stepped inside and nothing was there that could have cast a moving shadow or creates any audible noises.

As we exited the room the EMF detector sounded again. Whatever was inside the room had moved into the hall.

We both were astonished that we had seen something soon full-bodied, with sound. But that something did not want to interact with us.

I just hoped we had caught it on IR.

After this Jason and I talked about buying the Bahr building and preserving it as a paranormal museum. But we were both poor and had very little money or financing options.

The cleanup and restoration would have been very expensive.

Later that night I reviewed the film and after slowing the video down we in fact, did manage to capture it. I posted it on YouTube. It is an amazing piece of evidence.

I spent more and more time at Central State. I would explore the buildings alone. The only thing I wouldn't do alone was enter the tunnel system.

I realized the dangers of tripping over something or running into creepers, or my flashlight losing power and being stuck down there.

My only regret is I stopped wearing breathing masks. Take my advice always wear protection. I have even greater breathing problems today because of my poor decisions here.

This location has shaped me as an investigator more than any other. I have heard other paranormal enthusiasts say that once they are attached to a location they can feel when something isn't right there. They know the ghosts and the ghosts know them.

It's true. The more I visited Central State

the bond between me and the residents there grew.

I needed to understand them better so I decided to take the Medical Museum tour. The tour guides will tell you, "There are no ghosts at Central State."

I just shrugged my shoulders and thought to myself if you only knew how many are actually here.

I felt the tour people were afraid to know.

The tour last about an hour and is excellent and very detailed. I highly recommend it.

You will learn all about syphilis and how there wasn't any cure. How syphilis destroys the human brain. How for many decades patients families would drop them off at Central State and basically abandon them to their fate.

What Waverly Hills Sanatorium was for Tuberculosis Central State was for the venereal disease: Syphilis.

The sad part is families would drop family members off for dementia and a list of any other embarrassing signs that they just needed to go away.

Central State Hospital was in effect a dumping ground for people that had no voice to speak for themselves.

A little history:

"The Indiana legislature authorized the establishment of a "hospital for the insane" as early as 1827, but actual construction of a facility was delayed for several years. The Indiana Hospital for the Insane finally opened in November 1848 with a total of five patients. At that time, the hospital consisted of one brick building situated on a large parcel of land of over 100 acres on Washington Street, west of downtown Indianapolis. In 1889 the hospital was renamed the Central Indiana Hospital for the Insane. After 1926 it was known as Central State Hospital, and by 1928, physicians cared for nearly 3,000 patients.

From 1848 to 1948, the hospital grew yearly until it encompassed two massive ornate buildings (one for male and one for female patients); a pathological department; a "sick" hospital for the treatment of physical ailments; a farm colony where patients engaged in "occupational therapy"; a chapel; an amusement hall complete with an auditorium, billiards, and bowling alleys; a bakery; a firehouse; a cannery manned by patients; and idyllic gardens and fountains.

The more ornate of the two massive buildings came to be known as "the Seven Steeples". This building, which housed female patients, was designed using the Kirkbride Plan for mental health care facilities.

The Kirkbride Plan refers to a system of mental asylum design advocated by Philadelphia psychiatrist Thomas Story

Kirkbride (1809–1883) in the mid-19th century. The asylums built in the Kirkbride design, often referred to as Kirkbride Buildings, were constructed from the mid-to-late-19th century in the United States. The structural features of the hospitals as designated by Dr. Kirkbride were contingent on his theories regarding the healing of the mentally ill, in which environment and exposure to natural light and air circulation were crucial. The hospitals built according to the Kirkbride Plan would adopt various architectural styles, but had in common the "bat wing" style floor plan, housing numerous wings that sprawl outward from the center.

For a half-century, these complex buildings and gardens housed mentally ill patients from all regions of Indiana. By 1905, however, the state had built mental health institutions in Evansville, Logansport, Madison, and Richmond, thereby relieving an overcrowded Central State Hospital of some of its patient load and leaving it to treat only those from the "central district", an area of 38 counties situated in the middle portion of the state. In 1950 patient population reached 2,500

By the early 1970s, most of the hospital's ostentatious Victorian-era buildings had been declared unsound and razed. The Men's Department Building had been demolished already in 1941. In their place, the state constructed brick buildings of a nondescript, institutional genre. These modern buildings and the medical staff therein continued to serve the state's mentally ill until allegations of patient abuse and funding troubles sparked an effort to forge new alternatives to institutionalization which, in turn, led to the hospital's closure in 1994."

-        Wikipedia.

This article and others like it do not tell the story of the hundreds of people deposited here due to dementia, venereal disease (which for that time there was no cure.) depression, and many other reasons.

Wealthy families used Central State as a place to hide family members who were considered as an embarrassment to the good family name.

The poor were also placed here. People were left here to wilt and to die.

Central State no doubt had its fair share of successes and good medical care. But what led to its closing in 1994 were lawsuits from patient's family members alleging patient abuse.

Any reason to believe that the abuses only existed in the 1990s?

The day came when I began to see on the news and read in the newspaper that Central State grounds had been sold and would be used to build apartments and a new park.

The area would be revitalized to bring in jobs and people into the plighted area.

The next time I visited the Bahr building the police presence was evident. Police, fire, and rescue were there practicing inside Evans and Bolton.

I drove under a thickly leafed tree that partially hid my vehicle and my friend and I got out. We entered the Bahr building and made our way down to the tunnel system.

We exited the tunnel in front of the former administration building and walked back to my vehicle. There sat a patrol car parked behind my vehicle. I could see the officer sitting in his car and I knew he saw us.

I walked around to his car window and he asked, "What are you doing here?"

"Just taking photos before everything is gone."

He then said, "I saw you two enter this building and I yelled at you two to stop but you ran off in the building."

I replied, "We didn't hear anyone yell or we would have stopped." Luckily, I had my camera hanging around my neck. My camera probably saved us this day.

After a few more intense moments he let us go. He was very professional and courtesy and warned us "Not to return here again."

He said, "You don't want to be inside any of these buildings when the wrecking ball comes crashing through their walls. We have instructions now to keep people out."

That was the last time I would be inside any of the buildings at Central State Hospital.

Sometime later I was sitting in my bedroom when a wave of emotion came over me. I was hit by many voices saying goodbye to me. I knew then Bahr building was gone.

A few days later I drove through the grounds and Evans, Bolton and Bahr were rubble.

The Lowe Hotel

Both my parents were born very near a small area near Robson, West Virginia. Every summer they would pack us up into my dad's station wagon and we would take the long ride to grandmother's house deep in the mountains of West Virginia.

This yearly event was always an exciting time for all of us. Even though my grandmother's house had no TV to speak of. She had a television just very poor reception.

Everyone spent their days hunting, fishing, catching frogs, fireflies, butterflies, or damming up the creek that ran through her front yard.

My grandfather was always the expert hunter and he would hang fox pelts from his woodshed. He was an expert with any gun but his favorite weapon was a handcrafted slingshot.

My grandfather would spend hours searching for perfectly round stones to use in his sling shot. When he encountered a Copperhead or Rattlesnake it had little chance against my grandfather. Kermit would simply grab his slingshot, choose a stone and pull back the band and let loose. The stone always striking the snake in the head crushing it and killing it.

Many people tried to match my grandfather's skill with the slingshot but none ever did.

I miss both my grandparents.

These were special and unique moments in my life.

One day we were returning home dad decided to stop and visit a small park near a river. Dad rarely stopped when traveling. A stop for dad meant going through the drive-thru at a Burger King.

I remember going inside a small cabin, that was filled with rifles and artifacts. Outside the cabin we saw a large paddleboat sail by and the park had a huge statue out front.

This was my first encounter with the legend of Chief Cornstalk.

During another visit, I remember it was late and we were sitting on a bridge and my parents were alarmed because the bridge was shaking. They were relieved when the stop light finally changed color so they could go and get off the bridge.

I remember both of my parents saying, "Someone needs to check that bridge."

It was the Silver Bridge at Point Pleasant, West Virginia.

A short time later the Silver Bridge collapsed.

A little background:

"The Silver Bridge was an eyebar-chain

suspension bridge built in 1928 and named for the color of its aluminum paint. The bridge carried U.S. Route 35 over the Ohio River, connecting Point Pleasant, West Virginia, and Gallipolis, Ohio.

On December 15, 1967, the Silver Bridge collapsed while it was full of rush-hour traffic, resulting in the deaths of 46 people. Two of the victims were never found. Investigation of the wreckage pointed to the cause of the collapse being the failure of a single eye bar in a suspension chain, due to a small defect 0.1 inch (2.5 mm) deep. Analysis showed that the bridge was carrying much heavier loads than it had originally been designed for and had been poorly maintained."

-      Wikipedia.

Point Pleasant has always had its fair share of tragedy and blood. There was Lord Dunmore's War, the murder of Chief Cornstalk, the Mothman, UFO sightings, and now the Silver Bridge collapse.

Many years would pass before I would be able to properly investigate this small town. I was only six years old when the bridge collapsed.

Once again I would team up with my nephew Jason for several early investigations at Point Pleasant. It was Jason who told me about the military igloos in the TNT area and the very haunted Lowe Hotel.

As you enter Point Pleasant and you drive into town it's very mellow. People here are moving at a slower pace. Despite the years, Point Pleasant retains its country charm. The interesting part is the paranormal hot spots are all along the river.

At the junction of Ohio and Kanawha rivers stands Tu-Endie-Wei State Park. This park marks the battle for Point Pleasant by militia from Virginia and native tribesmen led by Chief Cornstalk.

Chief Cornstalk would later be murdered by locals when he entered the fort to talk peace.

If you continue down Main Street you will come to the Lowe Hotel.

A little history from a web page I found:

"The Lowe Hotel was opened sometime between 1901 and 1904 and was called the Spencer Hotel.

There are many stories about ghosts at the Lowe Hotel. The mezzanine between the first and second floors is home to one of the most famous of the Lowe ghosts. Such as a beautiful, but disheveled young woman is seen dancing to music only she can hear. She is barefoot, wearing a nightgown, and has long, flowing hair. It is rumored that she is the ghost of Juliette Smith, Homer Smith's middle child, and only daughter. As a young woman, Juliette loved music, and she loved to dance. She had fallen in love with a local boy, but her father disapproved of the marriage. The boy went on to marry another, while Juliette never did marry.

On the second floor, a small child between two to three years old is seen riding a tricycle. Most often the child is seen as solid as a real person and is so concentrated on her ride that she makes no eye contact or interaction with witnesses. Other times, only the sounds of laughter or the squeak of tricycle wheels is heard. It is generally felt that the child is a residual imprint of one of the Lowe children who lived and grew up in the hotel.

The third floor is perhaps the most active. The first of such is perhaps that of a former maid. Guests and employees have heard someone whistling when no one is around, and report a sudden chill and sense that someone is watching them.

Transoms over the doors are often found in the opposite position than that in which they were left, and cleaning supplies are found lying around where no employee has been to clean. Further, the cleaning products and supplies are never the brand or type that is used by the hotel staff.

The next third-floor ghost is that of Captain Jim, who resides in a three-room suite, probably 316. Captain Jim was first reported in 2005 by a woman staying at the hotel during a local festival. She had returned to her room to find a man standing, looking out the river towards the river. She asked him his name and what he was doing. He replied that his name was Captain Jim and that he was waiting for a boat. At this time, the woman noticed the man had no legs, and quickly fled the room. Research shows that a man by the name of Captain James (Jimmy) O'Brien was a captain for the Homer Smith steamboat in 1915.

Also on the third floor is a man with a beard and wearing 1930s style clothing. He is seen frequently in room 314.   A witness later brought back a postcard bearing the picture of Sid Hatfield, the Matewan police chief who was gunned down in McDowell County in 1921, and claimed he was the man she saw. There is no record that Sid Hatfield ever stayed at the hotel.

-       Theresa's Haunted History of the Tri-State.

Jason and I would stay here twice before I would eventually get married to Debbie and she would become my full time paranormal partner.

Jason and I spent our first night there touring the building trying not to be noticed. We took photos, videos, and conducted ghost box sessions.

Our room was straight across from the linen room. That night we kept hearing someone turning the linen closet light on and off. It was late and we thought, "Who the hell keeps going into the linen closet?"

We grabbed a chair inside the room to look out the window above our door and we saw nothing. No one was there. As soon as we would stop looking the light switch would click again. Another quick look by us and no one was there.

At one point we came out of our room and no one was there. We entered the linen room and no one was there. Was a ghost playing a mind game with us?

The next time we stayed at the Lowe it was me, Jason and another friend. We stayed in room #308. This other friend became violently ill and I was sure we would have to leave.

But eventually her symptoms calmed down and we were all able to sleep. I don't think whatever was there liked her cavalier attitude.

Debbie Enters the Fray

After visiting and investigating the Lowe with Jason I knew where I wanted to take my soon to be wife. I wanted to take her to the haunted Lowe Hotel.

She had been asking me to take her on a paranormal investigation. The truth is I was considering leaving the paranormal at this point. Meeting Debbie reinvigorated my interests in it and we became a mighty team.

Debbie had shared with me a few of her paranormal experiences from her childhood.

"When I was four we lived in a house that

we always called the Confederate House. I remember this little old lady wearing clothing from the mid-1800s, long sleeves, wearing a hoop dress all the way down to the floor. Her hair was dark and she wore it up in a bun.

This little old lady would always visit me in two rooms there. The two rooms were what I called my play room and we had a side porch. When I was alone she would come and visit with me.

She always seemed attracted to the really old piano that was in one of the rooms. I would play on the piano and she would sit right next to me.

I never saw her mouth move but it

seemed we would talk telepathy. I can't remember if she had a name.

I also felt a man was there but I never actually saw him.

She continued to visit me in those two rooms until we moved out four years later.

I think the reason that my siblings or parents never saw her was because they were skeptics. I told mom about the old woman who would visit me and mom thought I was crazy."

Another story Debbie shared is:

"I was about ten and I used to go with my babysitter and her daughter to her place of employment. Eventually, my sitter got a job at a mortuary fixing hair and makeup for the deceased inside the mortuary.

I remember my sitter being in her twenties and a real spiritual individual.

One day we were inside the mortuary, down the hall, by the stairway, in the room where the bodies are made up.

And my sitter was working on this deceased person's hair. When my sitter looked up and out towards the stairs and said, "You need to stop standing there and go away."

I start looking around wondering if my sitter is talking to me.

Then my sitter said, "Don't pay attention if

you see the lady standing on the curve of the stairs."

So I looked right up the stairs and there she was. A lady dressed in a blue dress, from the late 1800s watching us.

My sitter spoke right to the lady on the stairs and said, "We will respect your space but you have to respect ours. You can't be showing yourself. You need to go back upstairs.

The lady on the stairs vanishes.

I had seen a ghost."

As I parked beside the Lowe I asked her if she could feel the ghosts inside.

Pausing for a moment, nervous and

unsure about what to expect, Debbie answered, "Yes."

The Lowe was about to change her life.

That night in our room we both felt like we were being watched. Debbie described a man in his mid to late thirties, wearing a hat, clothes from the early 1900s and having a mustache.

She thought he may have killed himself.

She also saw a half body apparition from the waist down when she was in the restroom.

That night the bathroom light switch kept switching from off to on to off.

The next morning I went out to my truck while Debbie went to the restroom on the first floor. Debbie came out and said, a loud, obnoxious lady went to the restroom but all the stall doors were locked.

Debbie said, "The ghosts here don't like her, so they locked all the doors. I was just in there and they were all open."

The next day as we were heading out again. I was again left out first carrying items to my truck. Debbie went back to the room to grab something. When Debbie rushed out with a big smile on her face. I knew she had an encounter.

Our room was on the second floor. She said as she exited the elevator a little boy followed her to our room door and then vanished.

She also felt a very negative spirit follow her back to our room.

We had brought a lot of paranormal equipment with us. But we didn't bring a ball. So we drove down to a Dollar General and purchased a ball to see if we could draw this ghost boy out and capture him on video.

Later in our room, we placed the ball on the floor and started to video. Debbie felt as though the boy was just outside our door watching everything. I told her to invite him in.

He was there and we knew it. I felt he didn't like the video camera. I turned it off and within a few moments the ball moved across the floor and we captured a voice after I asked, "Do you want to kick it?"

The male voice answered, "I do."

We captured it on EVP and I posted it on YouTube.

It was an amazing moment for us.

The night before we left we were doing a cleansing asking any spirits that wanted to go into the light to please go. They had nothing to fear and everything they wanted or needed was in the light.

Something dark and menacing didn't approve.

As we walked the second floor it attacked Debbie. This dark male energy was foul and violent. I felt it rush around me and go right after her. Debbie's face turned pale and all the energy left her body. We had to return to our room so she could recover. It was frightening.

This would not be our last encounter with this dark male energy. He was very angry because we were cleansing his area and releasing some of the other ghosts that he had been lying to and holding captive there.

In our room, we continued to tell those ghosts that wanted to go into the light to please go. In a little while, the room felt different. The room became lighter and brighter as though a heavy veil had been lifted.

We stepped into the hall again and it was much brighter. The dark energy was still in the same area but he was much weaker and seemed weary of us.

We did notice that he followed us from behind as we walked the halls.

Debbie held me close because she was afraid after her first encounter with this dark energy. She was sure that during his life that he hated women and was probably a murderer. Perhaps, even killing a female in the linen room and hiding her body there?

When I returned home I listened to the EVPs we collected during this trip. When I got to the recording from the attack on Debbie, I became sick and was sure I would throw up. I bent over in my seat. The energy even from the recording was foul.

I haven't listened to that recording since.

Our next trip to the Lowe Hotel was another in your face experience. As we entered our room I started to set out REM Pods and prepare for an investigation.

I told Debbie something is over by the refrigerator. She walked over there to place items in the refrigerator and the REM Pod sounded and this ghost jumped on her.

It startled her so bad that she wanted to leave.

I rushed over to her and we sat on the sofa in the room to compose. As we sat there Debbie felt someone's fingers stroking her neck and shoulders in an amorous way.

At this point, Debbie was about to lose it.

Then she finally said, "Enough, you need to back off."

I'm not sure who was more surprised, me or the negative ghost who was probably sure he had her about to run.

The room we were staying in was known for an aggressive male spirit who liked to jump on females. Room #314.

After Debbie yelled at him, this ghost calmed down and left her alone.

Later in the evening, we could hear the people in the room beside us, blasting their TV, and talking loudly, so we asked this ghost to go torment them.

We believe he did.

The next morning as we were heading out,

we met our neighbors from that room talking about how they were up all night, terrified by an unseen force inside their room.

The Lowe Hotel gave birth not only to our marriage but also a new paranormal partnership.

Each of us different in how we approach the paranormal. Debbie is her own way more open to ghosts and their messages, emotions, etc.

It was exciting to have a partner that loved investigating as much as I do.

So many times I have seen Debbie become the trigger object for ghostly encounters. I don't know if it's because she works in hospice or if it's because she is an attractive female. Perhaps it's her ability to connect with them on a spiritual level?

The one thing I do notice is that we fill each other's void in the paranormal investigation field. What one lacks the other provides.

Debbie is more cautious. I am the one who will charge in and take on all things friendly or dark.

A Distant Memory

Years ago my dad who was an Apostolic Minister had a small church on Keystone Avenue in Indianapolis, Indiana. We had services there every Wednesday and Sunday.

My dad was very strict is in beliefs and remained that way until his passing many years later.

One night at church dad asked if anyone needed prayer please come and form a prayer line.

A small group of people slowly formed a single line and my dad begins to minister to each one individually.

There was a young girl there. She was a friend of mine. She was maybe sixteen or seventeen.

She nervously approached the altar area and my dad, and she began to shake and cry.

I had seen others crying but this was different. Something was happening and it was weird.

Dad must have seen something because he called the elders of the church closer to him and they surrounded this young lady and within a moment a deep male voice screamed out of her "Leave me alone!"

Her face changed, her eyes sank into her face and became fixed like a snake while turning dark black. It was no longer my friend there but something else.

The male voice yelling, "Leave her alone she is mine!"

My dad and the elders grabbed her. I ran up and I helped to hold her.

She was very strong.

I remember looking into her black eyes and it wasn't her anymore. Something else was looking back at us.

This struggle continued for several minutes with prayers being said over her.

A struggle, then calm, then struggle again.

Eventually, we laid her on the floor of the church where she began to wiggle on the floor like a snake with her tongue going back and forth.

It was frightening to watch.

Dad anointed her with Holy Oil and asked the entire church to pray with him, and suddenly whatever had possessed this young lady, lifted from her.

She seemed unaware of the events that had taken place over the previous hour or so.

Her face had a bright light about it. A light that it didn't have before. She was different, peaceful. Perhaps the first time she felt peace in quite a while.

The reason I am retelling this story is that in the paranormal field, everything is negative or declared a demon or demonic.

What my friend had inside of her was a demon. It was out to destroy her.

She weighed maybe 100 lbs and pushed five men around like it was nothing.

She spoke in a deep male voice that didn't sound human.

Her face and eyes changed.

If it had the power it would have killed us.

Later I learned through others she had been a victim of sexual abuse for years. This is probably how the demon gained entry.

Another encounter with the demonic was when I was called to go and cleanse a house. I knew nothing about the location or the people.

When I arrived, I was told by the lady that lived there, that her husband had gone hunting in the woods and had a seizure and died.

After that, her son being grief-stricken took one of his dad's guns walked into the backyard of the house and killed himself.

As I walked around on the main floor I felt the husband was still in the house watching over his wife.

She was in great distress and not willing to let him go on into the light.

As I walked upstairs, I could feel the son's ghost. This wasn't just a suicide. Another entity was there.

I went back downstairs, and the lady's daughter begins to tell me that after her father's death, teenagers had gone into the basement and conducted séances trying to conjure spirits.

I asked where the basement entrance was.

The young girl showed me, and I asked her to wait upstairs. As I headed down I became dizzy and disoriented almost to the point of losing my balance and becoming sick.

I wasn't ready for a confrontation yet.

I went back upstairs and made everyone leave the house because I didn't want any distractions.

Emily and I headed downstairs and she also felt dizzy and after a few moments, she left.

As I searched the room I saw a thing about three feet tall over by the gun case. Once it realized that I could see it, it split itself into two, with each part running in a different direction and disappearing.

It was hiding but still there.

I started to pray because this battle wasn't mine, but God's. This thing was invited in by teenagers fooling with things better left alone. This thing had attached itself to the young man who had killed himself in the backyard.

I knew from the Spirit, this was a weak feeder type entity that attaches itself to a living person and drains all hope from that victim.

I started the cleansing ritual. At one point I could feel my legs buckle, and I was sure I would be very ill.

"You have to leave. You are not welcomed here. You are an unclean spirit. I ask the Heavenly angels to come and forcefully remove you."

This went on for quite some time.

Then just like that, the heaviness lifted and it was gone.

Now I had to convince the lady of the house to let her husband and son cross over into the light.

They were there because they knew the danger from this entity.

She sat down in the living room and I asked her please tell them that you're alright now and you need for them to go into the light.

She started to cry.

Refusing to even consider it.

After a while, she told them both please go into the light.

She repeated it several times and suddenly the house felt different. A light of love had entered into her home.

Emily and I then saged and prayed through the whole house before I left.

If you ever encounter a demonic or dark spirit; never show fear because it feeds them.

Never engage in conversation with a demonic entity. They are liars and the truth is not in them.

So tonight, while you're watching a ghost show on TV realize that what they are calling demonic activity probably isn't.

When you bump into a demon you will know it!

An example of a false demon and a big reason why I no longer do home investigations is, I got contacted to do a home cleansing for a lady who shall as always remain nameless.

A friend of mine joined me on this cleansing.

We investigated the house and found nothing dark or demonic. We cleansed the house just to make the distraught lady happy.

Once I got back home she had sent me several cell phone videos of her sitting in front of her TV filming what amounted to dust flying in the air. She called these dust particles demons!

I received hours of these videos.

Later she even sent me a blurry photo of what looked like one of her kids wearing a

Satan's Halloween costume which she said was proof a demon was in her house.

I finally had to stop all contact with her. She needed help for mental illnesses, not a paranormal investigator or a cleansing.

Myself and others asked her to seek out a good therapist.

I have learned to trust my spiritual, emotional, and physical instincts when dealing with people and the paranormal.

Sedamsville Rectory

Sedamsville Rectory located in a quiet Cincinnati neighborhood is as rich in history as it is in paranormal activity.

Debbie and I have been to this location twice and we can verify this place is haunted.

The building in extremely elegant and a real treat just to walk through. The Catholic Ministers and nuns that worked here and lived in this area must have enjoyed such a beautiful location.

Debbie and I found that the basement has a lot of negative energy and something lives down there that doesn't want to be bothered by people.

While we were down there investigating, we both could hear audible growls.

At times the growls were intense and seemed directed right at me.

Nevertheless, I was determined to enter every corner of the basement and take photos and video.

I have learned that human ghosts will growl if you invade their territory.

In the Rectory basement, you absolutely realize that something or someone is right there with you.

One time I took a recording of dogs fighting and played it to see if I could get a response.

I had heard that dog fighting had taken

place in the basement after the Rectory was abandoned.

After I got home to review the recording nothing was there. Whatever was in the basement had either erased the recording or kept it from being recorded.

The main floor feels pretty normal and isn't nearly as active as the basement or upstairs.

The upstairs has a definite male presence and is almost friendly but gives you that private feeling.

We were more interested in drawing out whatever was downstairs hiding in the basement.

We returned to the main floor and

entered what I called the Library room. There we sat up REM Pods, the Ovilus 5, and a laptop to run an SCD1 session hoping to make contact.

At first, nothing happened.

Other investigators were there and we could hear them moving about.

Then, I said, "To the entity or ghost in the basement that growled at me and has been following me around come into this room and show us what you got."

A slow moving shadow creeped along the hallway wall, along the library door frame and finally into the room. Then boom all our equipment died. The room was heavy and oppressive. This thing was right there with us.

The laptop battery was completely drained out. Ovilus was dead. Nothing worked.

Creepy as hell.

That was our cue to call it a night and we packed up and headed home.

I was not ready for a paranormal or a demonic battle. I felt this thing had been egging me on the whole time and I wasn't falling for it.

It all started with me exploring the basement and ignoring its growls.

The Congress Plaza Hotel

The Congress Plaza Hotel in Chicago, Illinois is notorious for being haunted. From its fabled stories of suicide, bootlegging, gangsters the Congress has seen it all.

Debbie and I decided to check this location out. We were curious to see whether the stories we read and heard about this place were true or like a good number of places we go to, complete myths or lies.

The Congress is a beautiful building. It is ornate but does show its age.

Our room was on the eighth floor which was known to be the floor that Al Capone enjoyed when he would stay at the Congress Plaza.

Our only regret was the hotel was abuzz with tourists and partygoers due to it being St. Patrick's Day weekend. Everyone was loud and sucking down alcohol.

We were there to investigate and to take in a paranormal bus tour.

We unloaded a lot of equipment, REM Pods, Mel Meter, SLS camera, video camera, etc.

While we were busy unpacking, one of the cabinet drawers slid open. I walked over and pushed it closed.

I walked away thinking nothing of it.

A moment later it slid open again. I

checked it to see if it was off track or off balance. I closed it again. This time I sat there and watched it.

I told Debbie something is going on here.

The Congress is known for ghosts opening and closing drawers.

While we were watching this drawer another drawer to our right slid open. It was freaky.

It absolutely caught our attention.

We turned our REM Pods on and started to film with the SLS camera.

We did capture an unknown moving image on the SLS camera inside our room. We were in Room #830.

The Congress Plaza Hotel was revealing itself to be very haunted.

Late that same night we took the SLS and a video camera to the 6ᵗʰ-floor to do an SLS sweep of the entire floor. We were interested to see if we could capture any evidence about the young mother who had thrown herself and her two children out of the building from there.

The story goes: In the 1930s, a young Polish mother came to Chicago with her two sons. She was supposed to wait for her husband to arrive and then they'd start their new life on the city's north side. He never came. The depressed mother threw herself and her children out of a 6th floor window to their deaths. However, the body of one of the boys never made it to the city morgue. He's thought to play tricks on guests staying on the 6th floor.

To our amazement near the fire escape, the SLS captured a moving image that seemed to beckon us to follow him out the window. Was this one of her children?

We also checked out the mysterious room #666. For some mysterious reason only known to the Hotel owners, this room has been sealed up and hidden away from the public.

Hotel security was very gracious to us as we strolled around with our equipment. It was obvious they are used to investigators patrolling their building.

If you plan on investigating this location it will take several nights. This hotel is huge.

We posted our findings on the Congress Plaza Hotel on YouTube.

Let There Be Light

Debbie and I share a growing passion for cemeteries. We love the art, the history, and the folklore surrounding each one.

We often investigate cemeteries to see if there is any truth to the legends.

One such cemetery is in Madison, Indiana.

This particular cemetery is named Springdale and is located along the

Ohio River in southeastern Indiana.

We visited this location to film and investigate the legend surrounding a statue created by George Grey Bernard for his parents; he named the statue "Let There be Light."

The legend goes that on Easter morning the statue's eyes will bleed. Also, if you walk up to the statue and kiss her feet she will step down from her pedestal and chase you from the cemetery.

The first thing we noticed is this statue is breathtaking. She is beautiful. I was in awe of her standing there as if blessing all those beneath her.

The Italian marble seemed to glow in the sunlight.

We watched as a couple walked up and a woman kissed the statue's feet.

We knew then the legend was well known and we wondered how often this same event played out.

We grabbed the Ovilus 5 and our drone because we wanted to film her from the air.

Immediately, the Ovilus died. The battery completely drained out.

We set up the drone, set up the home coordinates and watched it as it lifted off.

We watched the drone video through my cell phone. The drone flew very close to the statue. We made sure to capture her from all angles.

The drone battery life is usually good for twenty to twenty-five minutes. In about twelve minutes the drone alarm sounded signaling low battery and the drone returned to its designated home point.

We packed the drone away and started our drive home.

Just outside of town we stopped at a gas station for a restroom break and snacks. I checked the cell phone video to see what we had captured from the drone and it was corrupted.

Once at home I pulled the SD card and downloaded the video directly into my computer. The file was there. But it would not play.

Had the statue or something inside Springdale prevented us from using the Ovilus 5 and the drone this day?

This was the only time video from the drone has failed to work properly.

Haunted Places

Debbie and I have visited and investigated so many locations. Waverly Hills Sanatorium, Whispers Estates, Gas Light Inn, The Guyer, Hartford City Jail, Poasttown School, The haunted Lowe Hotel, The Congress Plaza Hotel, The Old

Crown Point Jail, Ashmore Estates, Bachelor's Grove, Stepp Cemetery, Central State Hospital, Fox Hollow Farms, The legend of the Goatman, The Hannah House, The Roads Hotel, Hayswood Hospital, Okie Pinokie Woods, Pukwudgies, Revenant Acres Farm, and so many more that I can't name them all.

We have learned that provoking doesn't work. In fact provoking may actually be setting yourself up to be harmed.

We take gifts and use kindness. We introduce ourselves and explain why we are there. We always say, "We are here to meet you. Please talk to us."

We never ever do any damage to any property we visit.

We have learned that if you visit a location several times and linger there the ghosts will warm to you and are more likely to reveal themselves.

When investigating go with fewer people and you will get a lot more activity. Too many people tend to ruin any real investigating and you will learn the ghosts do not like it.

Imagine a group of twenty suddenly crowding into your home and asking you to perform.

I am always amazed when investigators freak out when a ghost yells at them to "Get Out!" or "Leave!"

Imagine strangers invading your home what are you going to yell at them?

Debbie and I have more paranormal equipment than we need and a lot more than we actually use. If you want to log activity I recommend the following:

Digital recorder

REM POD

Digital camera with video capability

K2

Wavepad or Audacity for cleaning EVP recordings

IR camera

Night vision lights

Flashlights

Lots of batteries

Patience

They Followed Us

We have had so many ghosts follow us home that it's almost expected now. Even when we tell them they need to stay where they are.

I don't know if it's because they're needy, lonely, confused or whatever. But if you investigate they will follow you home.

The signs are pretty obvious:

Feeling like you're being watched

Seeing shadow figures

Feeling uneasy

Hearing disembodied voices

Nightmares or weird dreams

Items being moved or disappearing

Pets staring into space

Being touched

Hearing a breath near you

Hearing footsteps

This problem is easily fixed by saging yourself and your entire house. These ghosts will run away from the sage so be sure to sage everywhere. We use white sage.

While saging tell them to go into the light, or at the very least, they have to leave you and your home and not return.

If you want you can open a door or a window and tell them to leave by that opening.

Do everything with love.

Is Death The End?

Every generation has asked is death really the end? Is there life after this human body dies? Paranormal Investigators everywhere are chasing answers. Every religion and spiritual person desires to know.

I choose to believe and my paranormal experience tells me that life continues.

But I will let Debbie close out this book with her own near-death experience.

"I was born with a heart condition that for years had gone misdiagnosed. Afib.

I was in the hospital.

This third episode put me into cardiac arrest.

I thought, "My God, I am going to die?"

Everyone was working on me.

Then I heard a female voice, almost like an inner voice say, "Just let go."

So I quit struggling and I let go.

Everything went black.

Suddenly, I could see again, I saw the people working on me.

I was in the air looking down on them and my body.

I thought, "Oh my God; I don't want to watch this anymore."

Everything went black again.

When I could see again, I was in this really beautiful green valley, full of flowers and a river. I was sitting there on a bench.

A woman was sitting on my right. I didn't know her.

My grandmother from Germany was sitting on my left.

I remember thinking I am dead because my grandmother was dead, but here she is.

I remember not feeling any pain, no heaviness, no sadness, and no anger.

I only felt joy and love.

It felt as though this joy and love came from inside of me and shot out in every direction.

Love without end.

I remember thinking I wanted to stay right there.

The lady on my right asked me if I wanted to stay or go back.

At first, I didn't understand her question.

Then my grandmother spoke up and said, "You need to go back."

I became upset because I had no desire to go back.

My grandmother spoke again, "You need to go back because you have children and they need you."

It dawned on me that the female voice that had told me to "let go" belonged to the lady who was sitting on my right.

I wondered if she was an angel or my spirit guide.

Then I remember a loud thump and feeling heavy as though I had fallen on to concrete.

I felt tears on my face.

I was back in my body in the hospital, and on my way to a slow recovery."

Final Thoughts

There are no paranormal experts. No expert mediums or psychics out there that can guarantee you contact with your deceased loved one.

But there are those rare moments when our loved ones come to us and they bring us hope, love and affection. They come to us in our thoughts, our dreams, a silent whisper or a memory.

The difference between an earthbound spirit and a spirit that has crossed over is quite simple.

An earthbound spirit is seeking something, searching for help, lost in a world that he or she is no longer a part of.

A spirit that has crossed over, is at full peace. When they visit us, they bring us a gift which is usually hope, love, or a message reminding us that everything will be alright.

As a paranormal investigator. we are not investigating spirits that have crossed over. These spirits are at peace and have little to no contact with us unless a loved one needs help or they become a guide.

We are investigating the earthbound
spirits that remain here for whatever
reason, so please do not believe
everything they tell you.